STATE CAPITALS

GALLERY BOOKS
An Imprint of W. H. Smith Publishers Inc.
112 Madison Avenue
New York City 10016

This edition first published in U.S.
in 1990 by Gallery Books,
an imprint of W.H. Smith Publishers, Inc.
112 Madison Avenue, New York, New York 10016

second printing

ISBN 0-8317-8833-X

Printed and bound in Spain

For rights information about the photographs in
this book please contact:

The Image Bank
111 Fifth Avenue, New York, NY 10003

Producer: Solomon M. Skolnick
Author: Thomas G. Aylesworth
Design Concept: Leslie Ehlers
Designer: Ann-Louise Lipman
Editor: Madelyn Larsen
Production: Valerie Zars
Photo Researcher: Edward Douglas
Design Assistant: Kristi Jo McKnight
Assistant Photo Researcher: Robert Hale

Every state has a capital city, where the business of state government is conducted. But no two state capitals are alike. They vary greatly in population, from Phoenix's 789,704 to Montpelier's 8,241. Some, like Lansing and Indianapolis, were carved out of the wilderness—created capital cities where no town had existed before. Some are old, some are young, ranging from Richmond (1607) to Oklahoma City (1889). Many states have had more than one capital city: Alabama, California, Georgia, and Tennessee had four, Rhode Island five, and Louisiana an impressive six.

Each state has a capitol building, or state house, where the legislature meets. These buildings come in an incredible variety of architectural styles. Some are "copies" of the U.S. Capitol in Washington, D.C.; some are Greek and Roman temples; and still others are skyscrapers. The capitols vary in age, from Maryland's venerable 1772 building to Hawaii's "recent" 1969 high-rise.

Here, then, is the story of capitals and capitols—a state-by-state exploration of yet another facet of our nation and its history.

Alabama, often referred to as "The Heart of Dixie," entered the Union on December 14, 1819.

Huntsville was the first state capital, followed by Cahaba (1820-1826), Tuscaloosa (1826-1846), and finally Montgomery (population 177,857) in 1846.

The Governor's Mansion, was built in 1900 of Alabama marble as a private home. The state bought it for the chief executive in 1950.

A memorial near the capitol building commemorates the fact that Montgomery was the first capital of the Confederate States of America in 1861.

Previous page: The State Capitol was completed in 1851 at a cost of $60,000.

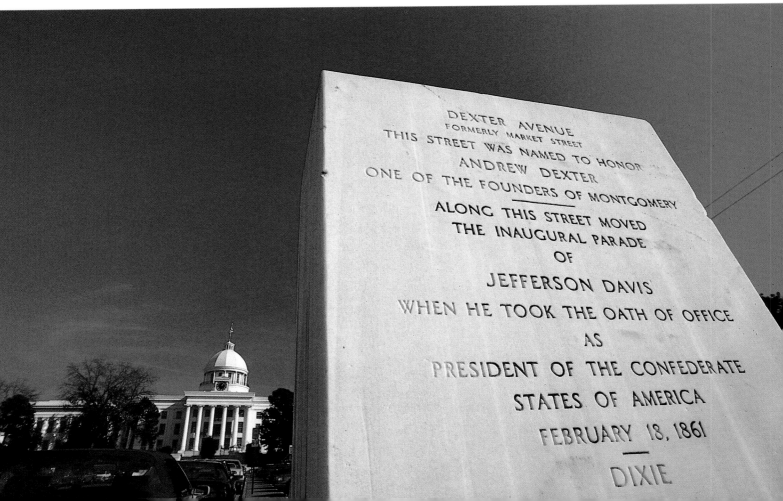

DEXTER AVENUE
FORMERLY MARKET STREET
THIS STREET WAS NAMED TO HONOR
ANDREW DEXTER
ONE OF THE FOUNDERS OF MONTGOMERY

ALONG THIS STREET MOVED
THE INAUGURAL PARADE
OF
JEFFERSON DAVIS
WHEN HE TOOK THE OATH OF OFFICE
AS
PRESIDENT OF THE CONFEDERATE
STATES OF AMERICA
FEBRUARY 18, 1861

DIXIE

"The Last Frontier"–Alaska–became the 49th state on January 3, 1959. Juneau (population 19,528) has always been the capital of the state.

The six-story capitol building was built in 1931 as the Federal and Territorial Building, and the state was given the structure when it entered the Union. Made of reinforced concrete with a brick facing, it has Indiana limestone facing on the lower two floors and Alaskan marble columns.

Juneau, situated along the Gastineau Channel at the foot of Mount Roberts and Mount Juneau, was named after Joe Juneau, one of the two men who discovered gold in the area in 1880–a discovery that started the first gold rush in Alaska.

Arizona, "The Grand Canyon State," joined the Union as the 48th state on February 14, 1912. The State Capitol in Phoenix (population 789,704) is a four-story, late Victorian style building. Completed in 1900 at a cost of $135,744, the outside is finished in three kinds of stone—granite, tuff stone, and malapai. It also houses the Arizona State Capitol Museum.

A variety of native trees, shrubs, and cactus plants surround the museum. Inside are a recreation of the original governor's office of 1912 and the early House and Senate Chambers. Nearby, in a place of honor, is the anchor from the U.S.S. *Arizona*, the battleship sunk during the attack on Pearl Harbor, December 7, 1941.

Arkansas (opposite), "The Land of Opportunity," became the 25th state on June 15, 1836. The State Capitol in Little Rock (population 159,159) was completed in 1916, and cost about $2.5 million. Made of Batesville marble and Indiana limestone, it was patterned after the U.S. Capitol in Washington, D.C.

California, "The Golden State," became the 31st state on September 9, 1850. Between 1850 and 1854, it had three state capitals—San Jose, Vallejo, and Benecia. Then, in 1854, Sacramento (population 275,741) was named the permanent capital.

The capitol building was begun in 1861 and completed in 1874. Constructed of stuccoed brick and granite, this impressive-looking building has Corinthian columns and a dome covered with gold plate. The copper ball on top is plated with gold coins!

Colorado was admitted as the 38th state on August 1, 1876, 100 years after the Declaration of Independence, and thus is nicknamed "The Centennial State."

Denver (population 492,686) has been the capital since statehood. Built on a ten-acre site, the capitol was completed in 1908 at a cost of almost $3 million. Resembling the U.S. Capitol, it is constructed from Gunnison granite, sandstone, and marble—all quarried in the state. The dome, 272 feet above the ground, is covered by Colorado gold leaf.

The colorful lighting of Denver's City Hall has become a seasonal tradition.

★ Connecticut is often referred to as "The Constitution State" because its delegates to the Constitutional Convention of 1787 worked out a compromise to break the deadlock over how many representatives each state should send to the U.S. Congress. One of the original 13 colonies, it became the 5th state of the Union on January 9, 1788.

Since statehood, Hartford (population 136,392) has been the capital city. The present State Capitol (upper right) was completed in 1879 and cost $2,532,524. Declared a national historical landmark, it is made of marble and has a gold-leaf dome.

The small and elegant Old State House, built in 1796, contains the restored senate chambers.

"The Sunshine State"—Florida (opposite)—joined the Union as the 27th state on March 3, 1845. The capital city is Tallahassee (population 81,548). The brick State Capitol was completed in 1845, and a copper dome was added in 1902. The 22-story executive office building behind it was completed in 1977. The awnings, a practical addition, give the building a home-like appearance.

★ Delaware is known as "The First State" because it was the first of the original 13 American colonies to ratify the Constitution. It entered the Union on December 7, 1787, and Dover (population 23,507) has been its only capital city. The state capitol building took many years to complete. It was begun in 1787 and not completed until 1792. To begin with, bricks from the old 1722 Dover courthouse were used for the brick façade of this Federal-era structure. The copper roof was added in 1795.

★ Georgia, "The Empire State of the South" as it's often called, was one of the 13 colonies, and joined the Union as the 4th state on January 2, 1788. Then the capital was Augusta, but in 1795, it was moved to Louisville, and then to Milledgeville in 1807. Atlanta (population 425,022) became the capital in 1868.

The capitol building, in a Classic Renaissance style, was built of Indiana limestone and completed in 1889. The dome is covered with Georgia gold, and topped by a 15-foot statue of Freedom.

The Governor's Mansion stands on an Atlanta hill. Built about 1910 of native Georgia stone, it was a private home until 1925, when the state bought it for the governor's residence.

The state capital of the "Aloha State" has been Honolulu (population 365,048) since Hawaii was admitted to the Union as the 50th state on August 21, 1959.

The Iolani Palace (above) was the seat of government from 1893 to 1969. This handsome Victorian building had been the home of Hawaii's royal family; the statue in front is of Kamehameha III, the king who united the peoples of the islands nearly 150 years ago.

The State Seal is displayed over the entrance to the new capitol, which is built of concrete and steel. Dedicated in 1969, the building rises behind an 80,000-square foot reflecting pool.

"The Gem State," as Idaho is often called, was admitted to the Union as the 43rd state on July 3, 1890. The capitol building in Boise (population 102,249), the capital city, was first used in 1912. It was designed in the same style as the U.S. Capitol, and it took 15 years to complete—at a cost of $2.3 million. The exterior facing is Idaho sandstone, and inside the structure there are vast quantities of marble facing. The dome, 208 feet above the ground, is topped by a solid copper eagle, and eight massive columns ring the rotunda and support the dome.

Illinois (opposite), "The Land of Lincoln," became the 21st state on December 3, 1818. The first capital was Kaskaskia (1818-1820). Then came Vandalia (1820-1839), and finally, in 1839, the present capital, Springfield (population 100,054). In 1888 the capitol was completed at a cost of $4.5 million. It is located on a nine-acre site. Statues of Abraham Lincoln and Stephen A. Douglas, two of the city's most famous citizens, are, fittingly, on opposite sides of the grounds.

The Lincoln Home National Historic Site in Springfield is at 426 South 7th Street. This was the only home that the 16th President ever owned, and he lived here for 17 years before leaving for The White House.

"The Hoosier State," Indiana, became the 19th state on December 11, 1816. The state capital then was Corydon, but in 1824, Indianapolis (population 700,807) became the capital city.

The capitol building was completed in 1888 at a cost of about $2 million. The Renaissance-style structure, four stories high, was constructed of Indiana limestone and contains over 12 acres of floor space. The top of the dome is 108 feet above the main floor.

The War Memorial in Indianapolis is a huge building built of Indiana limestone and granite and dedicated to the Indiana citizens who gave their lives in American wars. The statue, "Pro Patria," is made of bronze.

Iowa, "The Hawkeye State," was admitted to the Union as the 29th state on December 28, 1846. At that time, Burlington was the capital, but in 1857, Des Moines (population 191,003) became the capital. The capitol building in Des Moines was begun in 1871, and was not finished until 1884, at a cost of $2,873,294. The foundation is of Iowa stone and Iowa granite. Missouri limestone and Anamosa were used elsewhere in the building. The central dome, covered in gold leaf, is topped by a lookout lantern with a finial that is 275 feet above the ground.

Kansas, "The Sunflower State," joined the Union as the 34th state on January 29, 1861. That same year, its citizens voted to make Topeka (population 118,690) their capital city. The state capitol building was not completely finished until 1903, although construction had started in 1866. Still, by 1870, part of it was put in use to house the legislature. The central part of the classical building is five stories high, and the wings are four stories. It is 304 feet to the top of the dome, on which is a statue of Ceres, the goddess of agriculture in Roman mythology. The building measures 399 feet north to south and 386 east to west.

The Commonwealth of Kentucky, "The Bluegrass State," was admitted to the Union as the 15th state on June 1, 1792. At that time, Lexington was its capital city. But in 1793, Frankfort (population 25,973) was made the capital.

The present capitol building was begun in 1905 and completed in 1909. The base of the exterior is Vermont granite, and the rest of the façade is Bedford limestone. The rotunda, the dome, and the lantern (212 feet from the terrace floor) were copied from the Hôtel des Invalides, Napoleon's tomb in Paris.

The Old State House in Frankfort, Kentucky's third capitol building, was completed in 1829 and used until 1909.

"The Pelican State," Louisiana, was admitted to the Union as the 18th state on April 30, 1812. From that time on, the state had a succession of capitals: New Orleans (1812-1830), Donaldsonville (1831), New Orleans again (1831-1849), Baton Rouge (1850-1861), Opelousas (1862-1863), Shreveport (1864), and New Orleans yet again (1864-1881). Finally the permanent capital was established in Baton Rouge (population 220,394) in 1882.

The present State Capitol, a 450-foot-high building surrounded by 27 acres of formal gardens, was completed in 1932. Massive sculptures, such as this one flanking an entrance, abound.

The Old City Hall (center) is in downtown Baton Rouge.

Maine, "The Pine Tree State," became the 23rd state on March 15, 1820 and Portland became the state capital. Augusta (population 21,819) was named the new capital city in 1832. The capitol was begun in 1829 and completed in 1832. After remodelings and enlargements, a dome, reaching 185 feet above the ground, was added. Atop the dome is a gold-leaf copper statue of "Wisdom."

★ Maryland, "The Old Line State" as it is often called, and one of the 13 original colonies, became the 7th state on April 28, 1788. From the beginning of statehood, Annapolis (population 31,740) has been the capital. The capitol was begun in 1772 and first occupied in 1779. The dome—the largest wooden dome in the country—was added in 1789. From November 1783 to June 1784, it served as the national capitol when the Continental Congress met there.

Annapolis was founded in 1649, and much of the town looks as it did long ago. Many fine old homes still survive on streets like Cornhill Street.

★ The Commonwealth of Massachusetts, nicknamed "The Bay State," was one of the original 13 colonies and became the 6th state of the Union on February 6, 1788. The state capital is Boston (population 562,994).

The State House overlooks Boston Common—formerly John Hancock's cow pasture. Completed in 1798, the building was inspired by ancient Greek and Roman temples.

Inside, paintings of historical interest line the walls of the loggias.

The Old State House (opposite) was built in 1713, and is Boston's oldest public building. The Boston Massacre occurred in the street outside it on March 5, 1770.

"The Wolverine State," Michigan, became the 26th state on January 26, 1837. Detroit was the first capital, and then in 1847 Lansing became the capital. Today, Lansing has a population of 130,414, but in 1847 there were no residents in the woods that were cleared to create a new city.

The State Capitol was begun in 1783 and completed in 1879 at a cost of $1.2 million. Located on more than an acre of land, the building is made of Ohio sandstone, Massachusetts granite, and Vermont marble. From the rotunda of the State House visitors can view the inside of the impressive dome.

Minnesota, "The Gopher State" as it is sometimes called, entered the Union as the 32nd state on May 11, 1958. Its capital city is St. Paul (population 270,230).

The present State Capitol stands on a hill overlooking the city. Ground for it was broken in 1896, and it was ready for occupancy in 1905 at a cost of $4.5 million. The lower part of the building was constructed of St. Cloud granite and the rest of the edifice of Georgia marble. The white dome is 223 feet above the ground. "The Golden Quadriga," pictured here, is at the south entrance to the Capitol.

"The Magnolia State," Mississippi, became the 20th state on December 10, 1817. The first state capital was Natchez (1817-1821). Then came Columbia (1821-1822), and finally, in 1822, Jackson (population 202,895).

The present State Capitol was completed in 1903 at a cost of $1,093,641. The neoclassical structure was built of Georgia granite and Bedford limestone. The dome rises to a height of 180 feet, and at the top is an eight-foot copper eagle covered with gold leaf. The massive bronze, "Our Mother," dominates the approach to the Capitol.

Missouri, "The Show-Me State," was admitted to the Union as the 24th state on August 10, 1821. The first capital was St. Charles, from 1821 to 1826, and then in 1826 Jefferson City (population 33,619) became the capital city.

The State Capitol was completed in 1879 at a cost of $1.2 million. This neoclassical structure covers more than an acre of ground and is made of Ohio sandstone, Illinois limestone, Massachusetts granite, and Vermont marble.

The mural shown in the House Lounge (right) is by Thomas Hart Benton, the great Missouri artist. The city honors the third President of the United States, Thomas Jefferson—after whom it was named—with this larger-than-life-size statue.

Montana (opposite), "The Treasure State," was admitted as the 41st state in the Union on November 8, 1889. The capital city is Helena (population 23,938). The State Capitol, completed in 1902, cost a modest $485,000. The exterior is made of Montana sandstone; the copper-covered dome, 165 feet above the ground, is surmounted by a statue representing "Freedom." When the wings were eventually added to the structure, they were faced with Jefferson County granite.

Nebraska, "The Cornhusker State," became the 37th state on March 1, 1867. It is the only state in the nation to be nicknamed after a university football team. In 1945, the state legislature decided to honor the University of Nebraska Cornhuskers.

Lincoln (population 71,937) is the capital city, and the State Capitol, made of Indiana limestone, houses the legislature. Here, too Nebraska is unique because it's the only state in the country that does not have both an Assembly and a Senate.

Nevada has a number of designations: "The Sagebrush State," "The Battle Born State," and "The Silver State." It was admitted to the Union as the 36th state on October 31, 1864.

Carson City (population 32,022) is the capital. The State Capitol, an imposing sandstone structure, was completed in 1871. Its cupola is 120 feet high.

★ New Hampshire, "The Granite State," the 11th of the original 13 colonies to ratify the United States Constitution, joined the Union on July 26, 1788.

Concord (population 30,400) has been the capital since 1808. The State House is the oldest State Capitol in the country in which the legislature uses its original chambers. Completed in 1819, granite quarried in the Concord area was used in its construction. In the 1860s the building underwent major changes.

★ New Jersey, "The Garden State," so-called for its vast truck-farm industry, was one of the original 13 colonies. It became the third state when it ratified the United States Constitution on December 18, 1787.

From 1775 to 1790, there was no capital city, but in 1790, Trenton (present population 92,124) became the capital. The State House is the second oldest in continuous use in the country. The original building was completed in 1792, and in the mid 1800's, major restructuring was undertaken.

New Mexico, called "The Land of Enchantment," was admitted to the Union as the 47th state on January 6, 1912.

Although Santa Fe (population 49,160) has been the state capital since 1912, it has a long history as a capital. In 1610 the Spanish made it a provincial capital. Santa Fe witnessed the government change from Spanish to Mexican in 1822 and then to American in 1846. Thus the city is the oldest capital in the country.

The State Capitol, completed in 1953, was built in the shape of the Indian Zia (sun) symbol. The old adobe structure (below), the Palace of Governors, is a federal building and the oldest seat of government in the United States.

★ One of the original 13 colonies, New York, "The Empire State," ratified the Constitution and joined the Union as the 11th state on July 26, 1788. The first capital was New York City, but Albany (population 101,727) became the capital in 1797.

The Empire State Plaza in Albany contains government offices as well as cultural and convention facilities.

The Governor's Mansion is located south of the Capitol. Built in the mid-1850s, it was originally a private home. The state bought it for the governor's residence in 1877.

The State Capitol was first occupied in 1879. This structure of various architectural styles is made of granite and has been declared a National Historic Landmark.

JAMES KNOX POLK
OF
MECKLENBURG COUNTY
PRESIDENT
1845 — 1849
HE ENLARGED OUR
NATIONAL BOUNDARIES

ANDREW JACKSON
OF
UNION COUNTY
PRESIDENT
1829 — 1837
HE REVITALIZED
AMERICAN DEMOCRACY

ANDREW JOHNSON
OF
WAKE COUNTY
PRESIDENT
1865 — 1869
HE DEFENDED
THE CONSTITUTION

★ "The Tar Heel State," North Carolina, was one of the original 13 colonies. It became the 12th state on November 21, 1789. From 1776 to 1794 there was no fixed state capital, but in 1794 Raleigh (population 149,771) became the capital city.

The Capitol building was completed in 1840 at a cost of $532,682. The exterior walls are made of North Carolina gneiss, and the columns are modeled after the Parthenon. The President's Monument at the Capitol honors the three Chief Executives who were born in North Carolina.

NORTH DAKOTA
CAPITOL

North Dakota, "The Flickertail State" as it is sometimes called, entered the Union as the 39th state on November 2, 1889. The state capital is Bismarck (population 44,485).

The Capitol—the "Sky-scraper Capitol of the Plains" as some say—was completed in 1934 at a cost of $2 million. The 18-story structure was built of Indiana limestone. Nearby is Avard Fairbanks' massive bronze, "The Pioneer Family." It honors those early settlers in the region whose bravery and spirit created North Dakota.

Ohio, "The Buckeye State," was admitted to the Union as the 17th state on March 1, 1803. Chillicothe was the capital until 1810, when it was moved to Zanesville (1810-1812). Chillicothe served as the capital again (1812-1816) before Columbus (population 565,032) became the final site. The present capitol building stands in a ten-acre park. It was completed in 1861—22 years after construction had begun. An annex, which was built at a cost of $450,000, opened in 1901. The capitol shows strong classical influence in its architecture.

LEARNING ADORNS RICHES AND SOFTENS POVERTY
Socrates

"The Sooner State," Oklahoma (opposite), was admitted to the Union as the 46th state on November 16, 1907. The original capital was Guthrie, but in 1910 Oklahoma City (population 404,014) became the capital.

The State Capitol was completed in 1917 in an area that later became a major oil field, and oil wells surround the grounds. This neoclassical building is made of Indiana limestone with a pink and black granite base. The total cost was about $1.5 million.

Oregon (opposite), "The Beaver State," was admitted to the Union as the 33rd state on February 14, 1859. The capital city is Salem (population 89,091). The present State Capitol was completed in 1939 at a cost of about $2.5 million. A four-story building, constructed of white Vermont marble and bronze, its massive tower bears an 8½-ton bronze statue, "The Golden Pioneer."

★ The Commonwealth of Pennsylvania, "The Keystone State," was one of the original 13 colonies. When it ratified the Constitution, it became the 2nd state on December 12, 1782. At that time, Philadelphia was the capital city. From 1799 to 1812 it was Lancaster, and finally Harrisburg (population 53,246) was named the capital. Construction of a new State Capitol was authorized in 1897, and work was completed in 1906. The neoclassical building of Vermont marble is five stories high and cost $10,073,174. Its dome, which reaches a height of 272 feet, is surmounted by a statue symbolizing the Commonwealth.

★ One of the original 13 colonies, Rhode Island became the 13th state on May 29, 1790. At that time, it had five capital cities at the same time—Newport, East Greenwich, Bristol, South Kingstown, and Providence. The number was reduced to two in 1854 (Providence and Newport). In 1900 Providence became the only capital.

The capitol, begun in 1895, was completed in 1904 at a cost of $3,018,416. The exterior is made of white Georgia marble. On top of the dome is an 11-foot high, gold-leafed statue representing "Independent Man."

★ South Carolina, "The Palmetto State," was one of the original 13 colonies. After approving the United States Constitution, it became the 8th state on May 23, 1788. Its first capital was Charleston, but in 1790 Columbia (population 101,229) was named the capital. The State Capitol (opposite) took over 50 years to build because of construction scandals and the Civil War. Authorized in 1851, it was completed in 1904. The granite edifice cost $3,540,000.

South Dakota, "The Coyote State," became the 40th state in the Union on November 2, 1889. In that year, Pierre (population 11,973) was named the capital city. The capitol was begun in 1907, and it was completed in 1910 at a cost of $1 million. The architect patterned this limestone structure after the capitol of Montana. Its dome rises to a height of 159 feet; 40,000 pounds of copper were used in the construction of the roof.

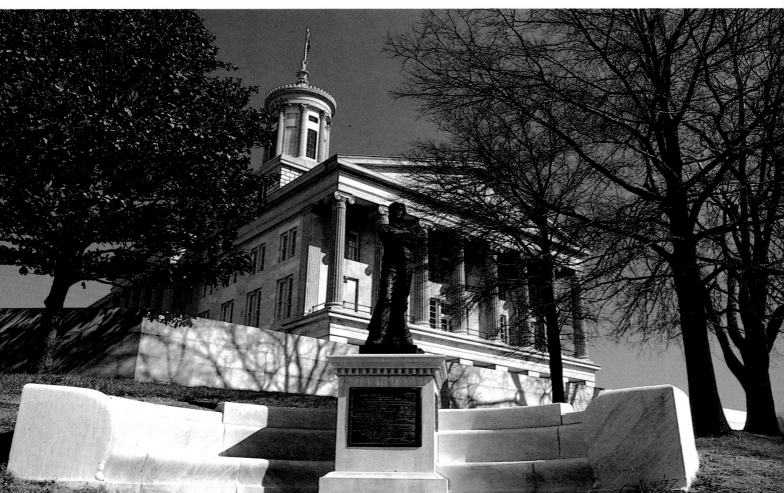

"The Volunteer State," Tennessee, became the 16th state of the Union on June 1, 1796. Knoxville was the first capital. In 1807, it was Kingston, and then Knoxville again (1807-1811, 1817), Murfreesboro (1819-1825), and finally Nashville (population 455,651) in 1826.

Not far from the capitol is the War Memorial (left), built to honor those servicemen who died during the First World War.

The Greek Revival capitol, made of Tennessee marble, was designed by William Strickland, a Philadelphia architect. The statue in the foreground is of Sam Davis, "The Boy Hero of the Confederacy." At 18, he was tried as a spy by a military court and offered a full pardon if he revealed the source of his information. Davis "would not betray a friend," and was hanged.

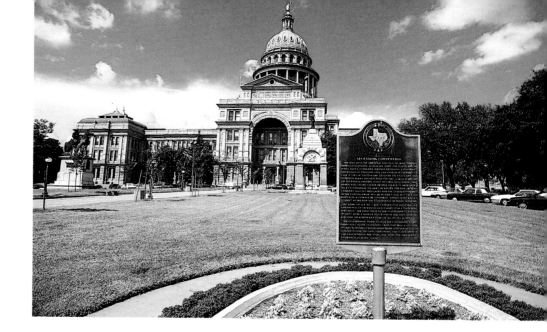

"The Lone Star State," Texas, became the 28th state on December 29, 1845. The capital city is Austin (population 345,890).

The capitol was begun in 1882 and completed in 1888, and is built of Texas pink granite. The dome, almost 310 feet above the ground, is surmounted by a 16-foot statue of Liberty. Near the capitol is a monument to the Southern Confederacy (center).

The Governor's Mansion, with its Corinthian columns and verandas, is an excellent example of antebellum architecture in Texas. It has an outstanding collection of art and antiques, and stands near the capitol.

Utah, "The Beehive State," became the 45th state on January 4, 1896. Salt Lake City (population 163,034) has always been the state capital.

The Renaissance Revival capitol building was completed in 1915 at a cost of $2,739,528. Its copper dome is 165 feet above the rotunda.

The Beehive House, now a National Historic Landmark, was where Mormon leader Brigham Young lived with his family. Built in 1854, this fine home also served as the first Governor's Mansion.

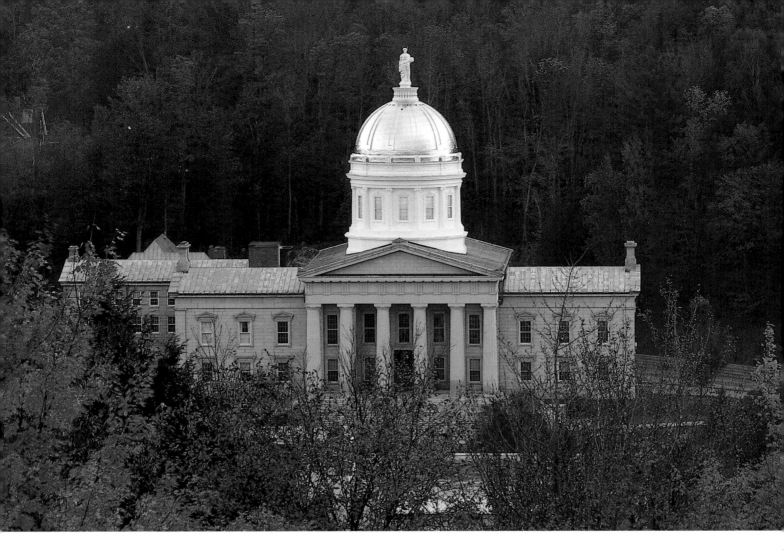

Vermont, "The Green Mountain State," became the 14th state when it entered the Union on March 4, 1791. Many towns served as the capital city before Montpelier (population 8,241) was chosen in 1808.

The State Capitol was completed in 1859. The exterior is finished in Barre granite, and the dome, 57 feet high, is sheathed in copper and covered with gold leaf. On top of the dome is a statue of Ceres, the Roman goddess of the harvest.

Inside the capitol, a marble statue of Ethan Allen (below) honors one of Vermont's great patriots. In 1775 he and the Green Mountain Boys captured Fort Ticonderoga from the British.

★ One of the original 13 colonies, the Commonwealth of Virginia— "The Old Dominion"—entered the Union on June 25, 1788 as the 10th state. Richmond (population 219,214) is the capital city.

The Governor's Mansion (top), northeast of the capitol, was built in 1813. The State Capitol (left) was designed by Thomas Jefferson and Charles Louis Clerisseau. The handsome structure is said to be the first building in America constructed in the form of a classical temple. The General Assembly first met there in 1788.

The Governor's Palace (opposite) in Williamsburg is a faithful reconstruction of the Royal Governor's residence. The town remained the capital of the colony until it was moved to Richmond in 1780.

Washington (opposite), "The Evergreen State," became the 42nd state on November 11, 1889. Olympia (population 27,447) has been the capital city since the state's admission to the Union.

The present State Capitol was built between 1911 and 1935 to replace the old wooden Capitol. Made of Wilkeson sandstone, the structure is 22 stories high. The dome, which rises 287 feet, is crowned by the "Lantern of Liberty." On the Capitol grounds is a monument to the servicemen of World War I.

West Virginia, "The Mountain State," once a part of the state of Virginia, was admitted to the Union as the 35th state on June 20, 1863. In the beginning, the state capital was Wheeling (1863-1870). Then came Charleston (1870-1875), Wheeling again (1875-1885), and finally Charleston (population 63,968) again in 1885.

The State Capitol stands on the north bank of the Kanawha River, and its 300-foot-high dome is surmounted by a golden eagle on a bronze staff. The structure was built between 1924 and 1932 at a cost of some $10 million. The exterior was constructed of limestone.

"The Badger State," Wisconsin, became the 30th state on May 29, 1848. Madison, its capital, has a population of 170,616.

Construction of the capitol (below) began in 1906 and was completed in 1917 at a cost of $7.5 million. Situated between Lake Monona and Lake Mendota, the Renaissance-style marble and granite structure (below) rises to a height of over 285 feet. Surmounting the dome—unique in that it is the only granite-domed capitol in the nation—is a gilded bronze statue, "Wisconsin," by Daniel Chester French.

Wyoming, "The Equality State," was admitted to the Union as the 44th state on July 10, 1890. Cheyenne (population 47,283) is the capital city. The capitol building (opposite), patterned after the Capitol in Washington, D.C., was begun in 1887 and completed a year later. Subsequently, wings were added in 1890 and 1917. The sandstone structure has a gold-leafed dome, 145 feet high.

Washington, D.C. (population 617,000), has been the capital city of the United States since 1800. In 1793 Thomas Jefferson proposed a competition for the design of a capitol (overleaf); Dr. William Thornton was paid $500 for his winning design.

The U.S. Capitol now stands 287 feet high from base to top and is 751 feet long and 350 feet wide. The cast-iron dome, which weighs 9 million pounds, is surmounted by the Statue of Freedom. This sculpture, the work of Thomas Crawford, was added in 1863.

More than just the place where the Senate and House of Representatives meet, the U.S. Capitol is an important symbol. Here Presidents and statesmen have lain in state, to be honored by the nation they served.

CAPITAL FACTS

ALABAMA   *Capital:* Montgomery
Entered Union & (rank): Dec. 14, 1819 (22)
Nickname: Yellowhammer State
State flower: Camellia
State bird: Yellowhammer

ALASKA   *Capital:* Juneau
Entered Union & (rank): Jan. 3, 1959 (49)
Nickname: The Last Frontier
State flower: Forget-me-not
State bird: Willow ptarmigan

ARIZONA   *Capital:* Phoenix
Entered Union & (rank): Feb. 14, 1912 (48)
Nickname: Grand Canyon State
State flower: flower of saguaro cactus
State bird: Cactus wren

ARKANSAS   *Capital:* Little Rock
Entered Union & (rank): June 15, 1836 (25)
Nickname: Land of Opportunity
State flower: Apple blossom
State bird: Mockingbird

CALIFORNIA   *Capital:* Sacramento
Entered Union & (rank): Sept. 9, 1850 (31)
Nickname: Golden State
State flower: Golden poppy
State bird: California valley quail

COLORADO   *Capital:* Denver
Entered Union & (rank): Aug. 1, 1876 (38)
Nickname: Centennial State
State flower: Rocky Mountain columbine
State bird: Lark bunting

CONNECTICUT   *Capital:* Hartford
Entered Union & (rank): Jan. 9, 1788 (5)
Nickname: Nutmeg State
State flower: Mountain laurel
State bird: American robin

DELAWARE   *Capital:* Dover
Entered Union & (rank): Dec. 7, 1787 (1)
Nickname: First State
State flower: Peach blossom
State bird: Blue hen chicken

FLORIDA   *Capital:* Tallahassee
Entered Union & (rank): March 3, 1845 (27)
Nickname: Sunshine State
State flower: Orange blossom
State bird: Mockingbird

GEORGIA   *Capital:* Atlanta
Entered Union & (rank): Jan. 2, 1788 (4)
Nickname: Peach State
State flower: Live oak
State bird: Brown thrasher

HAWAII   *Capital:* Honolulu
Entered Union & (rank): Aug. 21, 1959 (50)
Nickname: Aloha State
State flower: Hibiscus
State bird: Nene (Hawaiian goose)

IDAHO   *Capital:* Boise
Entered Union & (rank): July 3, 1890 (43)
Nickname: Panhandle State
State flower: Syringa
State bird: Mountain bluebird

ILLINOIS   *Capital:* Springfield
Entered Union & (rank): Dec. 3, 1818 (21)
Nickname: Prairie State
State flower: Violet
State bird: Cardinal

INDIANA   *Capital:* Indianapolis
Entered Union & (rank): Dec. 11, 1816 (19)
Nickname: Hoosier State
State flower: Peony
State bird: Cardinal

IOWA   *Capital:* Des Moines
Entered Union & (rank): Dec. 28, 1846 (29)
Nickname: Hawkeye State
State flower: Wild rose
State bird: Eastern goldfinch

KANSAS   *Capital:* Topeka
Entered Union & (rank): Jan. 29, 1861 (34)
Nickname: Sunflower State
State flower: Sunflower
State bird: Western meadowlark

KENTUCKY   *Capital:* Frankfort
Entered Union & (rank): June 1, 1792 (15)
Nickname: Bluegrass State
State flower: Goldenrod
State bird: Kentucky cardinal

LOUISIANA   *Capital:* Baton Rouge
Entered Union & (rank): April 30, 1812 (18)
Nickname: Pelican State
State flower: Magnolia
State bird: Pelican

MAINE   *Capital:* Augusta
Entered Union & (rank): March 15, 1820 (23)
Nickname: Pine Tree State
State flower: White pine cone and tassel
State bird: Chickadee

MARYLAND   *Capital:* Annapolis
Entered Union & (rank): April 28, 1788 (7)
Nickname: Free State
State flower: Black-eyed susan
State bird: Baltimore oriole

MASSACHUSETTS   *Capital:* Boston
Entered Union & (rank): Feb. 6, 1788 (6)
Nickname: Bay State
State flower: Mayflower
State bird: Chickadee

MICHIGAN   *Capital:* Lansing
Entered Union & (rank): Jan. 26, 1837 (26)
Nickname: Wolverine State
State flower: Apple blossom
State bird: Robin

MINNESOTA   *Capital:* St. Paul
Entered Union & (rank): May 11, 1858 (32)
Nickname: North Star State
State flower: Showy lady slipper
State bird: Common loon

MISSISSIPPI   *Capital:* Jackson
Entered Union & (rank): Dec. 10, 1817 (20)
Nickname: Magnolia State
State flower: Magnolia
State bird: Mockingbird

MISSOURI   *Capital:* Jefferson City
Entered Union & (rank): Aug. 10, 1821 (24)
Nickname: Show-me State
State flower: Hawthorn
State bird: Bluebird

MONTANA   *Capital:* Helena
Entered Union & (rank): Nov. 8, 1889 (41)
Nickname: Treasure State
State flower: Bitterroot
State bird: Western meadowlark

NEBRASKA *Capital:* Lincoln
Entered Union & (rank): March 1, 1867 (37)
Nickname: Cornhusker State
State flower: Goldenrod
State bird: Western meadowlark

NEVADA *Capital:* Carson City
Entered Union & (rank): Oct. 31, 1864 (36)
Nickname: Silver State
State flower: Sagebrush
State bird: Mountain bluebird

NEW HAMPSHIRE *Capital:* Concord
Entered Union & (rank): June 21, 1788 (9)
Nickname: Granite State
State flower: Purple lilac
State bird: Purple finch

NEW JERSEY *Capital:* Trenton
Entered Union & (rank): Dec. 18, 1787 (3)
Nickname: Garden State
State flower: Purple violet
State bird: Eastern goldfinch

NEW MEXICO *Capital:* Santa Fe
Entered Union & (rank): Jan. 6, 1912 (47)
Nickname: Land of Enchantment
State flower: Yucca
State bird: Roadrunner

NEW YORK *Capital:* Albany
Entered Union & (rank): July 26, 1788 (11)
Nickname: Empire State
State flower: Rose
State bird: Bluebird

NORTH CAROLINA *Capital:* Raleigh
Entered Union & (rank): Nov. 21, 1789 (12)
Nickname: Tar Heel State
State flower: Dogwood
State bird: Cardinal

NORTH DAKOTA *Capital:* Bismarck
Entered Union & (rank): Nov. 2, 1889 (39)
Nickname: Sioux State
State flower: Wild prairie rose
State bird: Western meadowlark

OHIO *Capital:* Columbus
Entered Union & (rank): March 1, 1803 (17)
Nickname: Buckeye State
State flower: Scarlet carnation
State bird: Cardinal

OKLAHOMA *Capital:* Oklahoma City
Entered Union & (rank): Nov. 16, 1907 (46)
Nickname: Sooner State
State flower: Mistletoe
State bird: Scissor-tailed flycatcher

OREGON *Capital:* Salem
Entered Union & (rank): Feb. 14, 1859 (33)
Nickname: Beaver State
State flower: Oregon grape
State bird: Western meadowlark

PENNSYLVANIA *Capital:* Harrisburg
Entered Union & (rank): Dec. 12, 1782 (2)
Nickname: Keystone State
State flower: Mountain laurel
State bird: Ruffed grouse

RHODE ISLAND *Capital:* Providence
Entered Union & (rank): May 29, 1790 (13)
Nickname: The Ocean State
State flower: Violet
State bird: Rhode Island red chicken

SOUTH CAROLINA *Capital:* Columbia
Entered Union & (rank): May 23, 1788 (8)
Nickname: Palmetto State
State flower: Carolina yellow jessamine
State bird: Carolina wren

SOUTH DAKOTA *Capital:* Pierre
Entered Union & (rank): Nov. 2, 1889 (40)
Nickname: Coyote State
State flower: American pasqueflower
State bird: Ring-necked pheasant

TENNESSEE *Capital:* Nashville
Entered Union & (rank): June 1, 1796 (16)
Nickname: Volunteer State
State flower: Iris
State bird: Mockingbird

TEXAS *Capital:* Austin
Entered Union & (rank): Dec. 29, 1845 (28)
Nickname: Lone Star State
State flower: Bluebonnet
State bird: Mockingbird

UTAH *Capital:* Salt Lake City
Entered Union & (rank): Jan. 4, 1896 (45)
Nickname: Beehive State
State flower: Sego lily
State bird: Seagull

VERMONT *Capital:* Montpelier
Entered Union & (rank): March 4, 1791 (14)
Nickname: Green Mountain State
State flower: Red clover
State bird: Hermit thrush

VIRGINIA *Capital:* Richmond
Entered Union & (rank): June 25, 1788 (10)
Nickname: The Old Dominion
State flower: American dogwood
State bird: Cardinal

WASHINGTON *Capital:* Olympia
Entered Union & (rank): Nov. 11, 1889 (42)
Nickname: Evergreen State
State flower: Rhododendron
State bird: Willow goldfinch

WEST VIRGINIA *Capital:* Charleston
Entered Union & (rank): June 20, 1863 (35)
Nickname: Mountain State
State flower: Rhododendron
State bird: Cardinal

WISCONSIN *Capital:* Madison
Entered Union & (rank): May 29, 1848 (30)
Nickname: Badger State
State flower: Wood violet
State bird: Robin

WYOMING *Capital:* Cheyenne
Entered Union & (rank): July 10, 1890 (44)
Nickname: Equality State
State flower: Indian paintbrush
State bird: Meadowlark

Index of Photography

All photographs courtesy of The Image Bank,
except where indicated*